Romey's Order

PHOENIX POETS

ATSURO RILEY

Romey's Order

THE UNIVERSITY OF CHICAGO PRESS

Chicago & London

ATSURO RILEY was brought up in the South Carolina lowcountry and lives near San Francisco. His work has appeared in *Poetry*, *The Threepenny Review*, and *McSweeney's*, and has been honored with the Pushcart Prize and *Poetry*'s J. Howard and Barbara M. J. Wood Prize.

The University of Chicago Press, Chicago 60637
The University of Chicago Press, Ltd., London
© 2010 by The University of Chicago
All rights reserved. Published 2010
Printed in the United States of America
19 18 17 16 15 14 13 12 11 10   1 2 3 4 5

ISBN-13: 978-0-226-71942-9 (cloth)
ISBN-13: 978-0-226-71944-3 (paper)
ISBN-10: 0-226-71942-1 (cloth)
ISBN-10: 0-226-71944-8 (paper)

Library of Congress Cataloging-in-Publication Data
Riley, Atsuro.
    Romey's Order / Atsuro Riley.
       p. cm. — (Phoenix poets)
    Includes bibliographical references.
    ISBN-13: 978-0-226-71942-9 (alk. paper)
    ISBN-10: 0-226-71942-1 (alk. paper)
    ISBN-13: 978-0-226-71944-3 (pbk. : alk. paper)
    ISBN-10: 0-226-71944-8 (pbk. : alk. paper)
    I. Title.
    PS3618.I5326R66 2010
    813'.6—dc22   2009025409

for BENJAMIN DAVIDSON

An order where we can at last grow up to that which we stored up as we grew.

Seamus Heaney

CONTENTS

ACKNOWLEDGMENTS

Grateful acknowledgment is made to the journals in which earlier (and in some cases quite different) versions of this work first appeared:

Poetry: "Campground," "Chord," "Clary," "Diorama," "Drift-Raft," "Drill," "Filmstrip," "Flint-Chant," "Hutch," "Map," "Nullaby," "O," "Picture," "Rage-Lodge," "Roses" (as "The Roses"), "Scroll," "Skillet," "Story," "Strand," "Tablet," "Turn"
The Threepenny Review: "Box," "Object," "Skin"
McSweeney's and *The McSweeney's Book of Poets Picking Poets*: "Bell" (as "The Bell")

•

"Picture" was reprinted in *The Pushcart Prize XXX: Best of the Small Presses 2006*, *McSweeney's*, *The McSweeney's Book of Poets Picking Poets*, and *Poetry Daily*.
"Drift-Raft" and "Chord" were reprinted in *Poetry Daily*.

•

The author wishes to offer his thanks to:

Poetry and the Poetry Foundation, the Unterberg Poetry Center of the 92nd Street Y, the Peninsula Artists Fund of Silicon Valley Community Foundation, the Greg Warren Fund
CA, BC, CK, ET
And especially Ben Davidson, Chris Kennelly, Kay Ryan, Christian Wiman, Frank Bidart for careful attention given to this work.

Romey's Order

FLINT-CHANT

Once upon a time a ditchpipe got left behind behind Azalea Industrial, back in the woods backing on to the Ashley, where old pitch-pines and loblollies grow wild. A mild pesticide-mist was falling and mingling with paper-mill smell and creosote oil the morning he found it. The boy shook and sheltered in its mouth awhile —*hoo-hoo! hey-O!*— and bent and went on in. It was like a cave but clean. He C-curved his spine against one wall to fit, and humming something, sucked his shirttail. He tuned his eyes to what low light there was and knuckle-drummed a line along his legs.

What the boy called inside-*oku* called him back. He was hooked right quick on the well-bottom peace of the pumicey concrete and how sounds sounded in there, and re-sounded. Tight-curled as he had to get —like a cling-shrimp one day, a pill-bug, a bass-clef, a bison's eye; an abalone (*ocean-ear!*), antler-arc, Ark-ant, apostrophe another— sure as clocks a cool clear under-creek would rise, and rinse him through, and runnel free. Hanging in a green-pine O outside were sun-heat and smaze and BB-fire and Mosquito Abatement. Inside there were water-limber words (and a picture-noisy nave), shades of shade.

PICTURE

This is the house (and jungle-strangled yard) I come from and carry.

The air out here is supper-singed (and bruise-tingeing) and close. From where I'm hid (a perfect Y-crotch perch of medicine-smelling sweet-gum), I can belly-worry this (welted) branch and watch for swells (and coming squalls) along our elbow-curve of river, or I can hunker-turn and brace my trunk and limbs —and face my home.

Our roof is crimp-ribbed (and buckling) tin, and tar.

Our (in-warped) wooden porch-door is kick-scarred and splintering. The hinges of it rust-cry and -rasp in time with every Tailspin-wind, and jamb-slap (and after-slap), and shudder.

Our steps are slabs of cinder-crush and -temper, tamped and cooled.

See that funnel-blur of color in the red-gold glass? —Mama, mainly: boiling jelly. She's the apron-yellow (rickracked) plaid in there, and stove-coil coral; the quick silver blade-flash, plus the (magma-brimming) ladle-splash; that's her behind the bramble-berry purple, sieved and stored.

Out here, crickets are cricking their legs. Turtlets are cringing in their bunker-shells and burrows. Once-bedded nightcrawling worms are nerving up through beanvine-roots (and moonvines), —and dew-shining now, and cursive:

Mama will pressure-cook and scald and pan-scorch and frizzle.

Daddy will river-drift down to the (falling-down) dock.

I myself will monkey-shinny so high no bark-burns (or tree-rats, or tides)

    or lava-spit can reach me.

I will hunt for after-scraps (and -sparks) and eat them all.

TURN

A bright-hot morning; me and Daddy; a fever-cloud of glassy-eyed iridescent flies. Up ahead, invisible heat-devils waver over our (brownbottle) boomerang of river; our rank-pink curves of bait-bucket chicken-neck marinate, and jellify, and stew.

We are walking the oyster-shell zig-path from my blood-home to the water, three hundred and eleven crunch-steps from back door to dock. This is Daddy's day off, our day for blue-crabbing. That neon hum you're hearing? —The colored jinks of flies.

They're all here today, every local-grown species, every flying insect with a taste for something spoiled: heavy-hipped houseflies and hairy-chested horseflies, bloated bluebottles, glossy greenbottles, dirtspeck-tiny screen-huggers too high-strung to swat. One minute back, they were hovering hairnet- (and halo-) style above my bald-headed daddy; now they are down-diving, and landing, in dark clots and clusters, on his eyebrows, neck-bones, knees.

Ninety-nine.

Along in here, our switchback crumbles down to shell-shards and powder.

One hundred.

His breath comes out vinegary when he turns.

Now he's the stagger-leggèd man, sun-squinting facing me so his eyes draw tight and Japanese like Mama's. He is fishing through the fly-fog for my name.

Romey-boy . . . he tries saying, slow-slurring it long, long, until the word-sound goes strange in the air and bends back on itself, like a shell-road or a river.

Ninety-nine.

Ninety-eight.

Ninety-seven.

The sand-bar has shown up (and shone) and I'm home-headed; that's my crab-net, and my lunch-bag, and my yellow fly-blown bucket, dragging there behind me like a ruined foot.

STRAND

Alphabet, sluice the porch.

Bind (and try to braid) our river-wrack and leavings.

Used to, it was cackle-berries and cat-heads with him when he dry-docked home.

Daddy: *Mama, don't cook all the running out them yellows!*
Me: *And raise them biscuits big, for sopping!*

Other egg-names of ours I've kept are hen-drops, and coop-mines (and -moons), and chicken-lights, and dumpties.

Here is the fillingstation-shirt he got from when he pump-monkeyed for money. The name-eggs (red-stitched and patched to where his chest would go) say *Eugene* on one side and *Esso* on the other. *Happy Motoring!* is tiger-tailed in script across its back.

Gas-smell's the main meat. Grass-sweat. Gnat lotion, neckwise. Ghost-whiffs of *GOOP* for gunky hands.

His hands (and mine, hammering) made this hutch. *I reckon your rabbit could use her a cabin or someplace. Chicken-wire's right airy, and cleans. Let's drive some stilt-legs down to set her up, so dogs don't help theirself to supper.*

(Instinct —*they can't hardly help it*— makes them try.)

Jim Beam & Jim Crow drive him through, like Jesus does some others.

Sure I'm evergreen for Wallace but I'm not no KKK.

Leaf. Leave. Leaves. Leaving. Left.

Have I said yet how mudworms (and flickery mind-minnows) live off leaf-chaff and blown bark-slough and home-grounds and gravel? *Son, rearing you some is easy: they durn nearabout feed theirselves!*

Time was —or truer, nights were— he'd porch-beach finally, or suddenly yard-founder, from nowhere.

One time I kerosened an ancient oak to lure him home.

POLAROID

The charcoal-stump of it.

The hole.

The rain-pond, ringed with turpentiney-smelling pines (and understory-birds)

and stinging vines.

My quail-call was *too sissy-high by half* but strong as his.

But his (El Camino, Evinrude) rooster-tail was taller.

—Across to the Sand-Bar, right regular. L. J.'s, up by Eight-Mile.

The Dock (On Tuesdays, 2 for 1). Smokey's Darts & Gristle.

There was the trestle that carried the train that trusted the trestle that bridged

the river that cooled the fish that fed the boy that watched the trestle that

slow-cankered and -rusted and fell.

Wadn't that your deddy we seen —hunching like a stray, Sunday last—

underneath the Upriver Overpass?

'Daddy' Eugene Hutto = verb.

(Plus, how to hammer, wire, and jerry homely words.)

Ex-anchored, for example.

Yesterdaddy.

Zags.

OBJECT

Her hair is double-dyed the same blackberry-shine as Mama's.

Her face is egg-sized, and white as White Lily flour.

If she was a baby-type doll, the kind that talks and whimpers, I would pull on her speech-string until it was frayed good and gray-greasy. I would bend down and press my ear against the speaker-holes in her body's (probably) pink plastic, the way a doctor would check your chest for heart-sounds, the way a landlocked child might listen for live ocean in a shell.

But she is a grown-woman doll.

Her hands are all but hidden in the wide wings of her kimono; a wide stiff sash —clabber-colored and freshly sewn (and bowed in back) by Mama— binds her hip-bones, belly, rib-cage, spine. She's not quite one foot tall. And since she's kept up there, on the highest shelf of our glass-faced china cabinet (*shiny cabinet*), I'm knee-teetering close on a corn-yellow kitchen stool, pen-lighting her parts in the knick-knack darkness, candling them like farmers scan their eggs.

Her feet are sure tiny. The one that shows could be a peony-petal come loose and fallen from the hem of her costume, where a peony-pattern —hand-embroidered, yard-accurate, nearabout microscopic— rises up off the fabric like braille.

The blade-pointed lines, of course, are leaves. And those spongy-looking thread-clusters stand for prize-winning blooms three years running, big as biscuits in real life and pale-colored like milk or mother-of-pearl. And those fine-stitched silk knots, scattered all over like bird-seed (or, bird-shot)? —They mean to say there are ball-buds everywhere. And how tight-sealed they are. And how the pinch-jointed ants are sometimes seen going slowly frantic over them in the side-yard, crawling over and over each hard-glazed casing, pacing and praying for some surface-craze or opening, feeler-tapping for some way inside the skins . . .

SKIN

Our kitchen-floor linoleum is pocked some and pitted, swollen in a few places and (mostly) off-pink as a leg.

Dawn is cracking, and Mama's fingering flour in a bowl.

Blisters cluster over there by the sink, owing to floor-slope and pipe-seep and spring-steady trickling: a mildew-map will sprout, and spread, and blacken there by noon.

Now she's working the lard in —and dribbling clabber from a jug.

Down here up close, I can study where gouges have been dug by the hard rain of hot dropped (or, thrown) skillets: that one's a raggedy rabbit's foot same as Florida, this fresh one could be a tepee (or Fuji, seething) or a neat-cut wedge of pie.

Heat is rising, knocking and popping in the stove.

Sometimes I nerve-hover hand-sized square to square, nick-naming (and mind-mapping) every burn-mark and blemish: *starfish, Utah, Pee Dee River; Africa, amoeba, mole-mound, quail.*

Mama's palm-patting and -smoothing a belly-white (*Bobwhite!*) swole of dough.

See those plum-dark marks, leading stepladder-style from her wrist-bones to her elbows? —She calls them her kitchen-tattoos. Come bedtime, she'll bleach-steep (and breath-dry, and flap-dry) and daub each one with a cold cube of yellow butter: *oven-mouth, biscuit-pan, chicken-grease spatter; pressure-cooker, pot-lid, pickle-rack, steam.*

My daddy's hammock-slung (sleeping) in that picture-frame, (plexi) glass-shielded from coffee-fumes and the cabinet-door slamming. He carries tattoos, too: his (the ones showing) are inked-on anchors and bird's heads, bluegreen as blood-veins.

Mine are pink mostly, brownish-purple, some red.

MAP

Daddy goes.

Trolling and trawling and crawfishing and crabbing and bass-boating and trestle-jumping bare into rust-brackish water and cane-poling for bream and shallow-gigging too with a nail-pointy broomstick and creek-shrimping and cooler-dragging and coon-chasing and dove-dogging and duck-bagging and squirrel-tailing and tail-hankering and hard-cranking and -shifting and backfiring like a gun in his *tittie-tan* El Camino and parking it at The House of Ham and Dawn's Busy Hands and Betty's pink house and Mrs. Sweatman's brick house and Linda's dock-facing double-wide and spine-leaning Vicki against her *WIDE-GLIDE* Pontiac and pumping for pay at Ray Wade's Esso and snuff-dipping and plug-sucking and tar-weeping pore-wise and LuckyStrike-smoking and Kool only sometimes and penny-pitching and dog-racing and bet-losing *cocksuckmotherfuck* and pool-shooting and bottle-shooting over behind Tas-T-O's Donuts and *shootin' the shit* and *chewin' the fat* and *just jawin' who asked you* and blank-blinking quick back at me and *whose young are you no-how* and hounddog-digging buried half-pints from the woods.

DRIFT-RAFT

Some nights, blank nothing:

The ice-box, milk-purling in the kitchen.

The eye-of-pine floorboards ticking, clicking, planking themselves cool.

TABLET

That in this moment there is life and food —Wordsworth

Epitaph the Viaduct Meat and Three.

Crayon down how it supper-called —glow-belling, gloam-knelling for appetites—
butterish-gold.

Cut-shape and mucilage a crepe (and crimple-paper) back-drape: of overpass-
overhang, splinch- and sunder-ditch of feeder-creek, its oaks.

Pedestal coax-cakes in window-glass.   Hillock fry-bird, golden-crusted.

> *We cook Good most every night!*
> *Everlasting Rolls cost extra.*

Draw us family-style —and lightsome— drawn inside.

Upright Daddy, payday-spruce (and dry today) as daddies;

blossom Mama, peach as mothers;

larklet me.

Keen-pipit *Snap-Beans, Pot-Beans, Sweet-Potato-Shoes; Collard-Bills*

(in Hock-Stock), Hoppin' John —and Okry Stew. Cabbage Pie,

Cymbling Fry, Crowder-Peas in Cream; Cornbread (Tea-Glassed,

Buttermilked), Streak-of-Lean & Creasy Greens!

BOX

These twigs stand for clothesline-pines. First thing back when our lot was new, Mama ax-hacked them naked of their lower limbs and switches. This scratch-piece of (variegated) yarn's in here for how she Cat's Cradle–rigged our trees with wire.

One hairy sprig of this packing twine could count for cracklings, queasy-carried. —I mean pigs' rinds, threaded on my neck like beads. Mama crystal-cut (and fried crisp through the night) and fine-needled at them like a jewel-kindler would, or a spider.

Q: —*What did you learn at the Superette?*

A: —*A fret-worked choker draws a crowd.*

Okra does, too. These dry-rattle BB-seeds are seeds of the time when her okra-crop grew giant. She'd pounded fish-heads into fertilizer-cups (and carved complicated water-grooves) and flooded us like a paddy. Dark groves rose like Vietnam bamboo. Cars came by to see her camouflage-green stalks going high as the house, and how the bristly-pointed finger-pods were not like food but human.

People pointed at all she'd raised. And long wood-sided neighbor-wagons idled and lingered. And one man leaned his whole self out, and white-flashed and -popped, and tossed his melting flash-cube. And Mama lifted up this skirt to hide her eyes.

NULLABY

The one time we saw local snow I laid some by for later.

Owl, here is what I make with what I saved:

A yard same as mine but

White white,

Vines and house and sweet-gums

Smothered.

A paper-doll hedge of

Snow-selves, all

Bald of ears and eyes.

STORY

Mama favors this closet for a cellar-hole because of the oceanwater-dark in here, and cool.

I know it like the shape of my head.

The brine-grained ham-body —hanging, for long-keeping, where the shirts should go— tastes of pinkwhelk-shells or brain-coral (pocket-squirreled by me and sucked for salt), or crying. Her boulder-bellied hoard-sacks of flour for biscuits (*White Lily*), cornmeal (*Red Leghorn*), and rice (*The Rose of Carolina*) offer cradle-coves and -crannies on the floor.

Pacifying moves in waves. Black blank as graves for the longest time can color-bloom and -school of a sudden, like a shelf-reef lured to mind (flush with jelly-lamps (*Ripe-N-Tite*), and pink-naked fish let loose) or pastures; calm green-grazing live-looking seahorses hovering can turn-tide to skittish (reared, and scattering) —or ash.

The shank-hooked heavy ham-shape is crustifying like a barnacled whale. The hall-clock's (black-cooped, but yellow) balsa-bird is claw-scritching *tock tock snick, tock tock snick* the latch and minute-wheels, recounting:

—*What was boy was ham was humpback was bowhead.*
—*Is beluga, smooth as milk-glass.*
—*Is breaching clear to blue so he can breathe.*

DRILL

Mama talks in this one.

Here's us, backing down our driveway's maze of red-dirt dog-legs, her at the wheel (with a fresh-forged license), me turned around navigating, the yard black-dark but flushed now (and now) and now with brake-lights, her Kool-tip flaring on every hard in-breath, river-reek and oil-scorch and marsh-gas mingling, our under-chassis (and rear axle, eyeteeth) chuttering due to roots and rain-ruts, our rust-crusting Rambler swerving and fishtailing and near missing trees.

At the mailbox, gears knock, gnaw, grind, find Forward eventually: we're missile-heading straight (more or less) for the LowCountry fairgrounds; here's us, late, loud, breaknecking her blue-ribbon hoard to the Fair.

Everything is home-made.

Not just our back-seat freight of gem-flame jelly-jars (slip-skin grape, beet, black- and blueberry, brunt-apple, seed-splacked fig) and payload of pressure-torqued pickle-jars (wrick-kinked banana-peppers, lethal hot-hat peppers, (green) tear-tomatoes, hairy okra, baby-dills in brine), but also the crazy-quilt safe-swaddling them, the gummed saliva-labels neat-naming them, my mama's name —hieroglyphical, grease-penciled, 'KAY' (KAZUE) HUTTO— branding lids.

Do you reckon tomorrow they'll put my picture in the paper?

Will somebody do a write-up when I win?

DIORAMA

The Blue Hole Summer Fair, set up and spread out like a butterfly pinned down on paper. Twin bright-lit wings, identically shaped (and fenced) and sized.

This side holds the waffled-tin (and oven-hot) huts of the Home Arts Booths and Contests, the hay-sweet display-cages for the 4-H livestock, the streamer-hung display-stages where girl-beauties twirl and try for queen. There's rosette-luster (and -lusting), and the marching band wearing a hole in Sousa. And (pursed) gaggles and clutches of feather-white neighbor-women, eyeballing us like we're pigs' feet in a jar.

> *I wonder does her boy talk Chinese?*
> *You ever seen that kind of black-headed?*
> *Blue shine all in it like a crow.*

This other wing (the one I'm back-sneaking, side-slipping, turnstiling into) dips and slopes down to low-lying marsh-mire: whiffs of pluff-mud stink and live gnat-pack poison, carnie-cots and -trailers camped on ooze. They've got (rickety) rides, and tent-shows with stains, and rackety bare-bulbed stalls of Hoop-La Game (*RING-A-COKE!*) and Rebel Yell and Shoot the Gook Down. Stand here, on this smutch-spot: don't these mirrors show you strange?

Crowds are gathering. Yonder there and down, the yolk-glow of a tent is drawing men on (and in) the way a car-crash does, or a cockfight sure enough, or neon. The ticket-boy's getting mobbed at the fly of the door.

No sign in sight, except for the x of the Dixie-flag ironed across his t-shirt.

I am bone-broke but falling into line.

The men upwind of me are leaking chaw-spit and pennies.

That, plus the eye-hunger spreading like a rumor through the swarm.

The rib-skinny doorkeeper's hollering: *bet now, bout's bout startin'!*

Over his shoulder, a ropy yellow light.

Also: circles of white tobacco-smoke, and bleacher-rows of (cooncalling) men who know my daddy.

—And there he is, up in front with some tall man, iron-arming two black-chested boys toward the ring.

Bait-boy

minnow-naked

(neck to belt)

chigger-bit and calamined:

powder-pinkish chalk-nickels

spackle-scales

nipple-jots like dimes.

Buckets (sperm-teemsome

silversides

(prime) tad-tails

creel-crickets

redworms);

cottonmouthy creek-prong

(marsh-musk,

trailer-husks)

wrong-water swale

(and back-slues)

back

beyond.

•

Lure-spoor of brack-beyond:

fox-tracks

slp thwp slug-muscles

gristle-snails

coarse boar-hairs;

rumor.

Trace of wild-man

ruts of root-man;

king-snakes

snipe-cocks

rock-skinks

snappers;

crink of boot-man

funk of shack-man;

fire-coals

leg-traps

tackle-pile

tires;

tar-paper

(belt-man, *salt-man*)

shorts-shuck

shack.

RAGE-LODGE

Salts and sugars slow-crust (and sharp-gemify) along meat-string in science-glass.

—My (craw-quartz) crystal cut-stone features fire.

SKILLET

Was mine-drawn,

Was pig-iron;

—Is a cast-heft

Fact.

•

Chokedamp's in it,

Born blackdamp.

Blood-iron

Ore-stope, lode-lamps,

Turnturbulating crubble-corf and -barrows.

Trace-tastes of (blast-furnace) harrow-smelt and pour.

Holds the heat hard.   Rememories flavors: no warshing.

Carks and plaques itself in layers, like a pearl.

CAMPGROUND

Deep river, Lord, I want to cross over into campground—
There is a balm—

It could be the Ark in here for all the birds (and bird-dogs), and flying squirrels, and turtles.

Sylvia Bell is rising (dark still), and risen, busy-noisy as a wren daring dawn, high-pitching some river (crossing-over) song with cast-iron inside it, re-neatening and -fluffling her nest of leaf-orange afghans, seeming now herself to fly (quick as she is in her rust-breasted housecoat), sweeping, wiping, sigh-singing all the while, rag-wringing, boosting up my morning-blood with a bandanna sugar-tit, patting me or my pallet on every clinkling fly-by (her wrist-charms chiming in my hair like change), putting her *tea kettle!* wren-sounds on for the crying marsh-wren orphans, hush-harboring the baby-naked flying squirrels with a babydoll's bottle, finger-stroking (and coo-cooing) them like they're hers, moon-howling at the (rising) sun in the hounddog style, (rousing and causing a four-dog choir to answer), rough-brushing their brown backs (brown as her hands) and hand-feeding them one at a time like there's no such thing as time, box-grating crisp lettuce-leaves for the box-type turtles, leaving them to lower their head-flap doors alone, finally broom-propping our door-screen open for easy cat- (and greenglass dragonfly-) passage, lighting now beside me on my quilt-cushioned croker-pad, panting some, forehead-beaded, resting where we're feasting on the floor.

•

Sylvia's salving my calf.
Her trailer-house on the inside is orange as an opened yam.

Last night she mangered me in bible-quilts on a croker-sack pallet.
I slept like something clover-kept and fed.

The smells hereabouts are bucket-milk and breakfast crossed with corn-crib and pasture.
My calf-patch is oblong like a yam.

Yesterday she said Come on through the door, let's get you good & homely.
Then I homed her in on where I'm torn.

I can make a yam breathe steam like a vented volcano!
Sylvia's salving my calf.

SCROLL

Vein-known (the sheer drawn-sung shape of her), but looked-for; evermore looked-at and lamping: Fuji-san as moon on every page.

In every (ivory) picture-pane. The boy took to night-gnawing and -nursing this old (folding-out) book of mountains, his mother's. He nosed, naturally, and licked at the milkish-mushroomy cover-threads. He finger-hankered, unfolding, for something, something, something. He 'read.'

Look! Mama's cradle-place. Pines. Lakes. Reeds. Cranes. Plum-blooms (pink-tendered leastways: cherry, could be) and willows. A blue-carved C of wave.

The boy (bellied-down, and trawling) traced and craved.

Pined-over, snow-necked, notch- (and nipple-) peaked; pointed-at —*That! So!*— and figured: Fuji, Fuji-san, Fuji-no-yama . . .

36

HOKKU

Loom a paned mull-cloth

of least-grains, seed-lamps, inklings.

—Mama's root-bed, gleaned.

PIECE-WORK

Once upon a summer-quilt, a girl-child. Kazue.

A chestnut-glossy ribbon. Kazue-chan —as parcel— trussed and passed.

Handed —more so as hot hibachi-coal— from cord-mother to (hired) milk-mother
to skin-folks, foot of Fuji.

Yasuji-san (she says

sometimes). *My cousin.*

Dug up, stole yams for me. War turnips.

Bokugo-time, halfed his rice.

Her rice-life now (river-oaked hereabouts) near-underground, with chopsticks.

Behind backs. Night-kitchened.

Black of the dirt-shed (quick) if Daddy's high:

> —*Act American!*

Oku = Clack-scrabbling in closets.

One closet (pitch-layered, like lacquer) for Japan-pairs and -tissue:

　(My-sized!) sandal-shoes, wooden and stilted.

　A wood-haunched (nutmeat-tiny) bear with a fish.

　Clinch-carved carp-couples, pick-intricate as pecans.

　Dish as koi (in fin-chipped china); koi as dish.

Shhhh is the center-sound —and her shelter-hole— in *Hi ro shi ma　mushroom*.

Minomushi —bag-worms— make hanging bag-rooms from leaves (and straw, and silk-spit glue) and seal themselves inside them.

Her (slipcased) bug-book shows one camouflaged as beech.

High peaches time our hill was white.   Like moons in trees.

We'd sewed and hung cocoons, each fruit.   For shade of course.   Of paper.

That.

Bokugo was this hole we dug we closed ourself inside it.

So.

Shhhhh.

BELL

The heard-tell *how her baby'd burned* downrivering and rippling.

Rill and wave of chicken/prayer/purlow murmuring back.

Brackwater cove-woods by her marsh-yard oak-creaking and -crying.

Mourn-cranes and eave-crow and crape-blinded windows keening black.

Raining; wrack.

The grieve-mother *Malindy Jean* porch-planking brunt and planging.

Breasting river (crossing-over) songs with cast-iron inside 'em.

The live heft-fact scorch-skillet willow-strung low and hanging.

Her heaving shovel-hafts and oars to make it ring.

FOSTERLING-SONG

Hadn't he come to us out from County Home

cleaved to a caul-swaddle

cloth (of coarse croker-sack weave)

he all the time plucked and wrung?

HUTCH

—by way of what they say

From back when it was Nam time I tell you what.

Them days men boys gone dark groves rose like Vietnam bamboo.

Aftergrowth something awful.

Green have mercy souls here seen camouflage everlasting.

Nary a one of the brung-homes brung home whole.

Mongst tar-pines come upon this box-thing worked from scrapwood.

Puts me much myself in mind of a rabbit-crouch.

Is it more a meat-safe.

Set there hid bedded there looking all the world like a coffin.

Somebody cares to tend to it like a spring gets tendered clears the leaves!

Whosoever built it set wire window-screen down the sides.

Long about five foot or thereabouts close kin to a dog-crate.

A human would have to hunch.

Closes over heavy this hingey-type lid on it like a casket.

Swearing to Jesus wadn't it eye-of-pine laid down for the floor.

Remembering the Garner twins Carl and Charlie come home mute.

Cherry-bombs 4th of July them both belly-scuttling under the house.

Their crave of pent-places ditchpipes.

Mongst tar-pines come upon this box-thing worked from scrapwood.

From back when it was Nam time I tell you what.

ROSES

The house with the nick- and snigger-name *Snort and Grunt.*

Shunned trailer-house, (pocked) scorn-brunt. Side-indented,

thorn-bined, boondocked in a hollow.

In a green-holler clamber-mire of itch-moss and bramble.

Tremblescent ditch-jellies, globberous spawn-floss. Drupes of

(dapple-clinkling) bottle-glass in trees.

Strangs them old oaks of his with NEHI *and liquor-pints. Magnesia!*

Yard-splayed magnolia-blooms, carved of tractor-tire. Milk-

painted (fangle-plaited) barbwire-scapes and -vines.

And -fronds. A palm-shape gold with birds at the end of the yard.

Elaborated branches, branching. What is fixing to be a rose-bush

caning and twining. Is leaves.

CLARY

Her cart like a dugout canoe.

Had been an oak trunk.

Cut young.   Fire-scoured.

What was bark what was heartwood: *Pure Char-Hole*

Adze-hacked and gouged.

Ever after (never not) wheeling hollow there behind her.

Up the hill toward Bennett Yard; down through Eight-Mile, the Narrows.

Comes Clary by here now

Body bent past bent.   Intent upon horizon and carry.

Her null eye long since gone isinglassy, opal.

—The potent (brimming, fluent) one looks brown.

45

Courses Clary sure as bayou through here now

Bearing (and borne ahead by) hull and hold behind her.

Plies the dark.

Whole nights most nights along the overpass over Accabee.

Crosses Clary bless her barrow up there now

Pausing and voweling there — the place where the girl fell.

(   )

Afterwhile passing.

Comes her cart like a whole-note held.

O

What was it for the longest time but lore, lure;

A heard-tell growing gold in the mind.

Word said (and word'd spread) it was well on back

Through the underwood by Bowen's Canal.

Past convoluted trees there's claydirt, a clear patch.

A (rife) clearing.

Ripe croodle-field.

Ring.

•

Bear off

Right where understory comes to grief entire—

Grubble this way head-down

Belly-down claw through clingburrs as a creature.

Cross (fret-morass and canebrake) and pass.

•

Encompassed here

Where springs not fail

Canes not break nor welt on backs of leg

Green cresses plait

No plaque of heated iron scathes

(Nor noose, nor knives)

Articulated scapes arise

•

Always the story-man lights lard-lamps in a circle and tells.

A boy scrapes and ever-graves for likeness with a stick.

Two girls croodle corn-songs cane-songs back and forth unbroken.

Once-bent bodies leap (in chorus) leg and whirl.

CHORD

Come the marrow-hours when he couldn't sleep,
the boy river-brinked and chorded.

Mud-bedded himself here in the root-mesh; bided.
Sieved our alluvial sounds—

•

Perseverating fiddler-crabs pockworking the pluff-mud;

(perforated) home-bank gurgle and seethe;

breathing burrow-holes, under-warrens, (pitched) pent-forts, coverts;

a rabbity heart-hammering amongst the canes;

bleat of something;

sleeping Mama grinding (something) with her jaw;

Daddy rut-graving gravel driving off;

the desolated train-trestle rust-buckling —and falling;

an echo-tolling cast-iron skillet like a gong;

downrivering *gone (gone) gone (gone)*;

Sylvia supper-calling her fish-camp fish with a bell;

putting her *tea kettle!* wren-calls on for the crying marsh-wren orphans;

R. T. tale-telling down by Norton's Store *"Where every Story cauls a Grief;"*

Daddy —*nine-eyed, knee-walking*— aisle-weeping at the Bi-Lo;

Mama mash-sucking sour loquats in the shed;

ire-salts quartzifying in the dark;

the caustics;

the fires;

far Fever Creek revival-tents hymning and balming;

bees thrive-gilding the glade;

hand-strang bottle-oaks (and intricated yardwire-works) clocking and panging;

Viaduct Forge & Foundry beating time;

the bait-boys along the dock drum-dunting their buckets;

vowel-howling over the water;

the river;

RIVER.

NOTES

ROMEY   Eye and voice of this book.

OKU   Japanese; roughly equivalent to interior, a deep place.

BOKUGO   Japanese; underground bomb-shelter.

HOKKU   In Japanese poetry, the initiating verse of renga or renku
               (linked-verse poems); also the verse element of haibun
               (verse-prose hybrid).

OCEAN-EAR   A not-uncommon nickname for the abalone, owing to its
               shape.

TAILSPIN   Brand of perfume.

CRUBBLE   Rubble, pebbles, scoria, slag.

CYMBLING   Cymling, a type of summer squash; cf. petticoat, pattypan.

HOPPIN' JOHN   New Year's good-luck dish of black-eyed peas cooked
               with rice.

CREASY GREENS "Creazy." A wild cress gathered along creekbanks and
               ditches.

SPLINCH   Split off, splinter.

EVERLASTING ROLLS Yeast rolls made rich and long-keeping with the
               addition of butter and eggs.

PURLOW   Pilau, perloo, perlow, purlo, pilaf—a common cooked-rice
               dish, a mixture.

CROODLE   To make a soft, low murmuring sound (to coo as a dove); the
               humming of a tune.

The book's epigraph is from "Crediting Poetry," Seamus Heaney's 1995 Nobel Prize lecture (*Opened Ground*, Farrar, Straus & Giroux, 1998).

"Tablet": The epigraph is from "Lines Composed a Few Miles Above Tintern Abbey" by William Wordsworth.

"Scroll": The books referenced are sequences of woodblock prints: Hokusai's *36 Views of Mt. Fuji* (1823–29) and Utamaro's *Picture Book of Selected Insects* (1788).

"O": The line "Where springs not fail" is a quotation from "Heaven-Haven" by G. M. Hopkins.

"Chord": The phrase "every story cauls a grief" is adapted from R. T. Smith's poem "Horton's Store" (*Brightwood*, LSU Press, 2003).